Walking Backward

poems by

Paul Lake

STORY LINE PRESS

1999

Published by Story Line Press, Inc.
Three Oaks Farm
PO Box 1240
Ashland OR 97520-0055
www.storylinepress.com

This publication was made possible thanks in part to the generous support of the Andrew W. Mellon Foundation, the Charles Schwab Corporation Foundation, the Nicholas Roerich Museum, the Oregon Arts Commission, the San Francisco Foundation and our individual contributors.

Book design by Paul Moxon
Watercolor by Tina Selanders Lake

Library of Congress Cataloging-in-Publication Data

Lake, Paul, 1951–
Walking backward : poems / by Paul Lake
p. cm
ISBN 1-885266-72-3 (alk. paper)
I. Title.
PS3562.A379 W
811'.54—dc21 99-22540
CIP

Walking Backward

SOME OF THESE POEMS HAVE APPEARED
IN THE FOLLOWING MAGAZINES:

Boulevard. "Thorn"
Carolina Quarterly. "A Grain of Salt," "Revised Standard Version"
Chelsea. "Eternal Recurrence"
Crosscurrents. "Two Hitchhikers"
Edge City Review. "Seeing the Elephant"
The New Criterion. "Pieces," "Simon Says"
The Paris Review. "The Century Killer"
Slant. "In a Parking Lot"
The Southern Review. "The Gift"
Sycamore Review. "Inspectors"
Texas Review. "Epitaph for a Draft Dodger"
Verse. "Concord"
Yale Review. "Additions"

I WOULD LIKE TO THANK ARKANSAS TECH UNIVERSITY
FOR A SUMMER WRITING GRANT THAT AIDED IN
THE WRITING OF THIS BOOK.

CONTENTS

Interrogations

Thorn

At the end of his chain—cold, solitary, straining
his throat with high-pitched barks, half-strangled yaps,
    night-shattering howls—
a neighbor's dog is testing
the limits of charity,
                                        leaning toward the house
where its owners are asleep—*would* be asleep
if its loud body-shuddering yowls would ever let up.

The house's windows are dark. Light,
sound might encourage the pup—
so the shepherd whines and rattles the light-gauge chain
that anchors him to the derelict pick-up truck's
back bumper, behind the rickety wooden shed
where they've penned him again, to deflect his nerve-
    twanging racket
away from their open windows and into ours. . . .

Not an hour, or a day, or a week, but every night now
that the old couple's grown-up children reside with them
in the small untidy rooms, crowded together,
children spilling out of the house into a van
stationed at the rear. The lawn's now a parking lot
of ancient, thundering sedans;
the clothesline flaps its flag of mute surrender.

These are the salt of the earth.

The patriarch
is eighty-seven. I see him staggering
all over town behind the rattling carriage
of a bladeless lawnmower, his dim eyes magnified
by thick lenses as he prowls the streets and gutters
for the flattened aluminum wafers he tosses up
to the collapsing cardboard carton on the empty chassis,
smacking his lips and gums with satisfaction
as he staggers ahead, eyes out for the next rubbish heap.

Winter or summer, his sons gather in the yard
with a hammer and anvil din, to wrench treadless tires
off unyielding iron rims, to slam hoods, bang doors . . .

with a vigor one could almost find admirable
if it were to some visible effect.

If in their eyes and the eyes of their wives and children
the specious beatitudes
of poverty weren't quite so manifest:

the mothers in shapeless gowns, the bad teeth, lean
bodies,
all those ineluctable longings and crippled dreams . . .

Whining, yiping, thrashing, half-strangled, loud—

fierce appetite left out in the cold autumn drizzle,

ignored, unignorable as it renews
its animal complaint—not quite

acknowledgeable thorn
lodged in the flesh,
whose point silences silence,

unneighborly test of our nerves and the neighborhood.

Inspectors

He said it smiling, one hand on the open door
To let the cold air quicken the invitation,
"You want to try your luck again at checkers?"
Then entered the trailer, his boots caked thick with
mud.

I didn't mind—the floor was already pebbled
With clods from my own boots, left beside the door.
I skated on the gritty linoleum,
Fetching the extra chair. Then we cleared a space
On the report-and-map-littered work table
To start a game.

"They're going to suffocate you
In this sardine can without a proper heater.
Make those cheap bastards hook you up a furnace
Or shut them down. Tell them you'll shut them down."

As usual, I lost the opening games,
But in the third kept my back row intact
And had him down two checkers. Hope made my heart
Quicken, so to fill the intervals
Between my moves, he cranked out conversation
About botched jobs and crooked contractors,
Leaning forward on one elbow above the board.

A half-smile creased his face above his beard.

"I can *smell* a crook. Twenty years ago I learned
To sniff a bastard out—" he touched his nose
For emphasis, still smiling cagily—
"Now all I have to do is sniff the air,"
Then he chuckled as if enjoying a private joke.

"The Bataan Death March—you ever hear of that?
That's where I went to school to study bastards—
You learned quick there which ones would sell you out.
After our march across that sweat-box island,
The Japs shipped us back home, like souvenirs.
That's what we were to them—living property.
It wasn't work they wanted out of us,
Though they kept up the pretense. How much work
Can men starved down to skeletons perform?
They got their satisfaction watching men
Once enemies brought down to animal level,
Then lower than animals, turning on each other.
After three years there I weighed eighty-seven pounds.
Sometimes I got so desperate with hunger,
I'd save dried kernels from their horses' shit
Until I'd filled a can, boil it, and eat.
Once in the saving mood, I rat-holed quinine
They gave us for malaria. When I had enough—
What I *thought* was enough—I swallowed it all,
But it only made me sick enough to wish
Some other skeleton would finish me,
Though no one had the heart to do the job.

"Three years of that. They finally made me foreman
Of a work gang, with three women under me—
Jap women. One, I planned on marrying
After the war, but after liberation
A first lieutenant took me in his office
And told me what a mistake I'd almost made."

He paused to study the board in thoughtful silence,
Then squinted, adding,
                                        "If I were back there now
And had to trust my life to other men,
Which one of us inspectors do you think
I'd trust my life with—try and guess his name."

I thought a minute, calling up names and faces.
"I'm not sure . . . maybe Duffy, Duffy Landers."

"That sneaky son-of-a-bitch?
                                                  No, guess again."

I tried another name. He seemed amused
Or scornful as I ticked off half a dozen,
So I tried to think what grim criteria
A survivor of a death-camp might employ—
What fatal tic or slant-wise look of the eyes
Might give the telltale sign of a fink or traitor.
Looked at that way, we all seemed half suspicious.
I wondered how I rated on the scale
He used to measure men, then gave up guessing.

"So what did you do when you got back to the States?"

His eyes wrinkled at the corners.
"Stayed in the
army.
And here's a funny thing that happened there
When I'd been home a while. This crazy buddy
Told me how we could supplement our pay
By playing guinea pigs at Edgewood Arsenal—
They had some kind of gas they had to test.
I thought, Why not—what could they do to me
I hadn't had done ten times worse already,
So we both signed up. I found out I was wrong.

"They locked us in a room with one glass wall,
Strapped on our masks, and then sat back to watch.
My buddy passed out first—the gas had leaked
Right through the mechanism—I woke up later
In the hospital, stiff as a wooden plank,
And for six months I couldn't twitch a muscle.
My buddy had it worse. He was paralyzed
For the best part of a year. But the worst news was
That after we could walk, we still weren't men
Entirely: Our peckers wouldn't stiffen.
They said that was a normal side-effect
Of nerve gas, but my buddy took it hard
And swore he'd marry the first girl with the touch
To make his flagpole stand up to the breeze.

I never saw a man so full of himself
The next year when I showed up at his wedding.
Now he's a colonel. I guess that goes to show
The kind of pricks they take for officers.

"So make your move. . . .
You've made it close this time,
I'll give you that.
You ever figure out
Which one of us inspectors that I'd trust
With the only life I'll ever have to live?
You're looking at him—that's the truth of it.
What say we have another go-around
After I pull this game out of the fire?
I'll put my boots on while you study it."

I moved a piece, then pushed my chair away
As things grew clear.

"Is that your move?" Now smiling,
He rubbed his palms together. "Go on, king me."

Walking Backward

You're wondering why I'm back in Minnesota—
I know it wasn't business that brought you here.
What business could ever get you to Bemidji
With its one gallery filled with Indian art?
Pots, blankets, beads . . . hardly your cup of tea.
You've come to put me on the straight and narrow
Runway back to Minneapolis,
New York, or Boston—anyplace but here—
And think that while you're doing me a favor
You'll do yourself one, too, but I won't go.
After so much trouble mastering the trick
Of walking backward, I can't turn around
As easily as that. I've come too far.
Instead, I'll tell you of a man I met
That might help me explain what brought me back
To my hometown against all sense and reason
After twenty years.

The fellow's name's Sam Harper.
I met him on the shoulder of the highway
Beyond the mall my first week back in town—
I passed him walking north as I drove south.
I *thought* that it was north. When I got closer,
I saw that he was walking in reverse,
Heel-first, in my direction down the highway,
Arms swinging at his sides so casually,

You'd think he thought that way was natural.
It was—*is*, I should say—at least for him.
Of course he once walked like the rest of us,
But took it on himself to make the change.
That's what he wanted when he started out—
To make a change. I spoke to him about it
One afternoon when he turned down our street.
It was unsettling the way we talked—
Him backing up, me walking straight at him
So that we kept a steady space between us.
I had the chance to study him up close.
He wore a string of sleigh bells round his shoulders
Which jingled with each step, and in one hand
Held a black plastic garbage bag, half full.
He told me that the sleigh bells were to warn
Pedestrians of his sudden blind approach;
The plastic sack he used to pick up litter,
Undoing others' damage where he passed.
It took more nerve to ask the obvious
Question about his walking, so I spoke
Quickly before it had the chance to misfire.
I'm glad I did. He never hesitated,
But softly, without shame or condescension,
Explained it with a biblical directness.
He said his life had gone so poorly forward,
He'd try the other way now for a change.
Though he kept his past a bit mysterious—
He'd done some time . . . he didn't say for what—
I doubt he'd ever maimed or killed someone.

If there'd been sins and wreckage in his life,
They didn't seem so radical in nature
As to make him turn his life around like that
In such literal fashion.

My next door neighbor
Explained that Sam is half Objibwe Indian
And half Norwegian, as if that might account
For the odd nature of his turnaround.
He didn't say which half gave the idea.
The truth is, no tradition Sam could hear of,
New World or Old, would urge such an odd course.
It came half-breed like him: He got it watching
That Dustin Hoffman movie, *Little Big Man*,
In which an Indian in a minor role
Walked, ran—even rode a horse—while backing up.
And yet, despite the comic origin
Of his self-imposed penance, Sam makes it seem
Right somehow. In another age we might
Have called it holiness and Sam a saint—
Now we dismiss it simply as eccentric.

That's how my own change came: Watching television.
One night I absent-mindedly turned it on
And found myself in 1968
Vietnam. Automatic rifle fire
Echoed in stereo around my room,
Raking the rubber fronds of jungle trees
As the sound-track rocked with recoils, trumpets,
shouts,

And a thatch-roofed village blossomed into fire.
Back then, of course, the actors weren't so handsome,
The pictures weren't so steady or so clear.
This was the dream of some vice president
Of network scheduling set in its slot
Of family viewing time to serve up action
In healthy dollops along with aspirin,
Tampons and deodorants. . . .

I turned the set off,
Then sat in silence for an hour or two,
Remembering how close I came to being
An actor in that scene—though, naturally,
Like all my friends—like all of both our friends—
Not only did I beat the draft myself,
I never knew a single man who didn't.
Those whose deferments were reviewed or lost
Still always somehow landed on their feet:
A friendly doctor said they were unstable—
I know an atheist who got deferred
On conscientious grounds, though he's no Quaker—
While others simply got a lucky draw
In the lottery or fled to Canada.
You won't believe how I avoided service.
I flunked my physical in perfect health.
By concentrating, I could raise my blood pressure
By thirty, forty points—I don't know how.
It's funny, isn't it? Then I felt clever,
And I suppose it was good luck, at that—

I didn't have to leave my native country,
Spend years in jail, or match my wits against
The skepticism of those staunch Lutherans
On my draft board in wild hopes of a C.O.
Instead, I got back on the Trailways bus
They brought us in on and went back to college
To learn to paint. They drafted someone else.
That's what I thought of that night as I watched
The blank-faced television—of that someone
Who went instead of me, that nameless other
Too dumb or forthright to resist, that boy
From my hometown or near it whom my draft board
Called up in its insatiable hunger
In my place and sent off to that foul war.

If I had done things differently—stood up
And borne the consequences at some cost
To peace of mind or body, I'd feel better—
Different, at least—though I'm not so naive
As to believe the wheels of that machine
Which gobbled up and crushed all those young bodies
Would boggle up its cogs on my account.
No wonder we keep turning back to it
In memory and television screenplays:
We want to give those times another ending,
To crown our acts with glory, find heroism
Where only the grim will to live survived.
Instead, we ought to put on bells and walk
Backward to collect the waste we've laid

As the frontiers of our monstrous egotism
Expanded. To contract our destiny
To the borders of some known and well-loved place
We might defend with courage, justice, honor.
I like to think that Sam might make it back
With all his walking, clearing us a path
Across an unlittered North America,
Where we might go, made festive by our sleigh bells,
Growing year by year more joyous with thanksgivings.

Pieces

The queen moves with unbounded liberty.
Slant-eyed, a bishop offers up a prayer.
A horse-faced gallant full of chivalry
Enters the family trade, an officer.

A rook, high as a silo, lets fire fall,
Then ends its run behind a remnant pawn.
The king strolls past his garden's rose-grown wall
To issue statements from the castle lawn.

Only the pawns, bald-domed as army ants,
Urged to the common good by stripes and prayers,
Regard the board, cursed with their consciousness
Of all the horror of those empty squares.

Epitaph for a Draft Dodger

Faced with a call to arms, he scorned those lies
That others packed like socks into their duffle,
Knowing that, winged by shot, no soul would rise
  Out of the scuffle,

That virtue was no shield with ghostly glamour
To blind an enemy or block a shell;
That cased in ego's large Vulcanic armor
  God-like Achilles fell.

Better, he thought, to slave, a hired man
For some dirt farmer, gnawing on wooden bread,
Than rule, a decorated veteran,
  Over the wasted dead.

Thus citing precedents, he made his choice,
Never to march in ranks, now forward, backward,
Except to shout with others NO MORE TROYS,
  Waving a placard.

Let others die. He traced memorials
Which like long roll calls named those gone to glory,
Then in prestigious periodicals
  Published their story.

Antigone

I wonder if you knew the sight you'd make,
Eyes bulging, bridal veil wrapped round your neck,
When Haimon, your fiancé, found you there
Locked in the vault where his own father placed you.
Did you intend for other hearts to break,
Seeing the awful bridegroom that embraced you,
Then one by one surrender to despair
And so before the king could grant reprieve
Abjure them all and take an early leave?

A clever girl, you always loved to flirt
With death, yet kept your virgin conscience clean
And even dying kept to vertical,
And none who saw you crouched on hands and knees
Above your brother's body, sprinkling dirt,
Would ever hint you did it to displease
The king, your uncle, whose tyrannical
Familiar jealous furies made you burn,
Seeing that man, that state, so stiff and stern.

Gauntlets

Dressed out, dressed down
respectively, in shining uniforms,
a thousand men are lined up
in two iron parallel files,
while one, a tall comrade-in-arms,
stands apart at the head of them, waiting.
Orders are, to club punch jab kick him
when he passes between the ranks,
and you'll do it, of course, those are orders,
however you feel personally.
It's the cumulative effect
does the trick—no one's guilty
when the victim comes stumbling out,
if he does, and your fault in it all
if he doesn't, is but one
tiny decimal,
if you want to grant any.

But supposing you won't,
when it's ordered, simply fall into line,
or, falling in, fail to strike
when the poor lout falls past—
well, then, here's the beauty:
It's your turn, my friend,
to run the gauntlet—your own
face throat thigh rib groin
finally bleeding or screaming
under the successive blows
of your former fellows.

What more economical
mathematical proof
of the total inefficacy
of love, trust, fellow feeling
has ever been worked out
to the mind's satisfaction?
It's a model of sorts
of community, really.
Though the heart might recoil
at such pitiless design,
who will violate orders
when the next president,
czar, premier, king, or führer
from on top the anthill
orders feet into line?

Interrogations

I

Let's start with the noisemaker's fife:
Trumpet, trombone, or oboe shaped,
It looks festive almost, like a horn,
Though your fingers are kept in their place
By a close fitting grip, and screwed down
Till they're locked to the fingerboard.
Imagine walking through your hometown
With that collar locked under your chin
And your fingers clamped in its vice
And the neighborhood children all laughing
And dancing as if to the tune
Of a vagrant Pied Piper too gay
To stop twiddling the stops or remove
The brass instrument from his mouth,
Whatever his current condition
Or mood of the gathering crowd.

II

What droll imaginations men had
To carve stocks out of iron and wood
In the shape of an instrument and
Then call it a neck violin

Or shrew's fiddle, to lock women up
So it looked like they fingered its strings.
What a jig those old girls must have stepped
At the end of a chain when dragged home.
Or should one give too much rein
To her tongue, she might suddenly find
Her head slapped in a cast iron mask
In the shape of a bird's or boar's head,
An iron bulb forced between her teeth
Like a bit in a horse's mouth,
And the shape of her world metamorphosed
By that grillwork to something grotesque.

III

What did men think a body was
To be treated like that. Where was soul,
So much spoken of, if not somewhere
In the flesh's interstices
They burned, flogged, or pierced with such pride,
As if rooting it out of its lair?
How trivial, how undignified
Even death must seem in a bronze bull
That's heated till, roasting inside,
A voice cries out in agony,
And bronze lips, to the frenzied delight
Of the crowd, howl, belch, bellow, and bray
Like a tormented animal.

IV

Death wasn't their object, nor pain,
Nor confession, whatever they said,
Those doctors and inquisitors of
Being's dark underground chambers.
Why string a man upside down
To saw him in half through the groin
If not to assure that some blood
Might continue to flow to the brain
To let him perceive all he can?
Why stake a man down to the ground
And then open him up with a knife
Just enough to clamp viscera
To a drum and then slowly turn,
If not to let mind reflect on
That unraveling knot, human life?

V

Rack, screw, Judas cradle, cat's paw—
The whole Medieval science of pain
Now seems paradoxical,
Recalling how such things were born
To crush the heretical doctrine
That matter and spirit remain
Locked in perpetual war;

That the body's so radically evil
That the soul must annul each dark cell.
What could those good fathers have done
To convince a heretical soul
Of God's love, of his perfect creation,
Except crush his bones under a wheel
Then weave the pulped limbs through its spokes
Before hoisting him up on a pole
To survey all His wonderful works?

VI

God himself set the precedent for
Every future inquisitor,
Argued one Ludovico, when He
Tried our first parents secretly,
Expelling them both from the garden,
Thereby seizing their worldly possessions,
Then condemning them always to wear
Fig leaves, like a green *sanbenito,*
Before handing them over to hell
To be purified in its fire.
St. Thomas himself theorized
That the purpose of man's resurrection
Was to make both our sorrow and joy
More intense, since in order to feel
Either pleasure or pain to perfection,
Souls need bodies as sounding boards.

VII

What could such a God mean to us
From his throne in impregnable heaven
Looking down on the torturer's prod,
Slaps, questions, the gun to the head,
And the victim's inscrutable writhings,
As He hovered above the world,
Sole witness, secure in the knowledge
Of his own immortality?
What hasty theological shotgun
Wedding of the spirit to flesh
Could effect a reconciliation
Of such a One to this variable world
He's supposed to have made and called good,
Unless mocked, beaten, and crucified,
He were finally, irrevocably left
Nameless, faceless, staring up at the sky,
Without credence, credentials, or creed
Among the other abandoned dead
On the road to the torture house.

Concord

To stop the wheels of state, I made
My life a kind of counter friction
And went to jail, my tax unpaid,
Until a friend with less conviction

Paid so its cogs might turn again
To spit me out. And as I stood
Behind those four thick walls of stone,
That heavy door of iron and wood,

I saw how states and institutions
Must be half-witted, thinking men
Are merely flesh and blood and bones
To be locked up at their discretion.

The night I spent in jail was novel
And interesting enough: My cell
Was clean and neat on my arrival—
It might have been a small hotel

The way the inmates leaned to chat
In doorways till the lockup call.
Once learning where to hang my hat,
I took my station at the wall

And gazed out through its grille, as pages
Of history seemed to waft my town
Backward to the Middle Ages,
Turning our Concord to the Rhine.

Next morning, through an oblong slot,
They passed our meal—brown hunks of bread
And steaming pints of chocolate—
And after having breakfasted,

My roommate, who spent mornings haying
In neighboring fields each day till noon,
Bade me good-bye and parted, saying
He doubted we'd be meeting soon.

Let out myself, I then proceeded
Across the street to fetch the shoe
I'd left to mend, then unimpeded
Strolled slowly down an avenue

And past the square and when last seen
On top a hill two miles from town,
Was lost in huckleberrying,
My conscience clear, my duty done.

Seeing the Elephant

Seeing the Elephant

I know you've only come
to see an old half-addled woman,
to wheedle out of me
what you've made up your mind to hear—
some tale to frighten children
or the child left in yourselves
to prove that, old as you are,
you can still shy away from something.
If that's all that you want,
go read the penny dreadfuls,
but bones and hide and hair
won't show you the elephant.

You're puzzled now. That's good.
Elephant, you think, what elephant?
There are those who think that elephants
don't belong in an account.
But who has ever set out
on a journey or a story
except to glimpse one, though
not everyone has seen it who
returns with a tall tale.

That's something I learned later,
remembering those loud young men

just back from the West who'd josh us,
laughing with open mouths
as we children whined and chafed
to be let in on the joke.
Then Pa caught the fever, too,
and teased us with it, saying
how we'd just up and see it
for ourselves, that elephant.

Soon, he'd commenced to building
our Pioneer Palace Car,
the two-storied covered wagon
such as no one on those plains
had ever seen the likes of.

It had
an entrance on the side
like an old-fashioned stagecoach
and two high-backed seats on springs
to ease the driver's ride.
Inside, was a little room
with a small sheet-iron stove,
whose vent pipe, running up
and out through the canvas cover,
was kept by a circle of tin
from setting fire to the roof.
And some of Mama's friends

added a looking glass,
in order, as they said,
that she might keep up her good looks.

Surely, no family
who ever crossed the plains
had started out their journey
better outfitted.
Even now
I can see our little caravan
of some ten or twelve covered wagons
full of Donners, Reeds, and children
as we set out from Springfield,
my little black-eyed sister
Patty, holding back the wagon cover
so Grandma Keyes—propped up
in her feather bed—might have
one last look at home.

We left that wagon standing
like a desert monument
just shy of the Great Salt Lake,
its mirror still unbroken,
and buried Grandma Keyes
in the shade of an oak, where now
Manhattan, Kansas, stands

next to the Big Blue River.
My little pony, Billy,
was cut loose like a boat.
I watched him growing smaller
until, seeming to sink
beneath an ocean of wildflowers
and grass, he went down,
still staring after us.

Not a hair nor hide of any
we left along the trail
survives now, except in memory,
and yet sometimes I ride
that dead pony into sleep,
jogging behind the wagon
blear-eyed, in a cloud of dust,
my ears full of the clatter
of hooves and wooden wheels.

You're growing restless now. Whose
garrulous, half-blind uncle
or tiresome grandmother hasn't
bored him with such a tale?
Covered wagons, Indians, crossings
commonplace as dysentery—

not a whiff of the elephant
in any of it, you think,
kept, as you are, by railroads
out of one's lumbering path.

Which one of you has seen
a father so kind and gentle
he'd never raised a hand
to discipline his own children
open another man up
like a seed bag, with a knife—
then when his plea of self-defense
was unreasonably denied,
scorned, scoffed at and,
without a map, food, or a gun,
banished from the camp
to face the wilderness, alone.
Following him into the dark,
I took him ammunition,
guns, and a loaf of bread,
clinging around his neck
till he pried me loose
and vanished.

That villain Lewis Keseburg
had turned the whole camp against him,

still angry about the way
Papa'd stopped him beating his wife.
For all his education and
his fine orator's voice,
even then a taste for human
flesh must have gnawed within.

Ah, now your ears prick up
like dogs' on a fox's path.
But if the wily fox doubles back,
the poor dogs are lost in circles.
Still, if you possess
a hunter's quiet patience
and a heart to follow the trail,
you might feel the hot breath
of larger game.

Last year
I came across one such trail,
shopping south of Market, when
I saw a familiar face.
Shaven-headed, squatting
cross-legged, begging for bread,
he looked more like a Chinaman
or a storybook Hindu than
a grocer's son out of Springfield.
Somehow I recognized him

after all those years, those changes—
Donald, I thought, Donald Jackson—
my tongue touched the familiar name.
Seeing the wistful look
he wore even as a boy,
I placed a silver dollar
in his outstretched bowl. I
knew what it was to be hungry.
Then chancing to catch his eye
as he turned his face away,
addressed him by name—"Hello, Donny,"
I asked, "Donny Jackson?"
But his look was impassive stone.

By now I was determined
to make him greet an old schoolmate,
and not knowing what else to say,
blurted out in a single breath, "Have
you seen it, Donny Jackson? Have
you seen the elephant?"

I might as well have spoken
to a cigar store Indian
for all the recognition he
gave in response. But then
a voice like a desert breeze
came out of the statue's mouth

and I had to listen closely
to catch it, I was so dumbstruck.

"A group of blind men," he commenced
to the best of my recollection,
"once came upon an elephant.
The first blind man felt the head
and declared it was like a waterpot,
but at the ears, another
said, 'No, it's a winnowing basket.'
'No, no,' shouted another, who handled
a tusk, 'it's a plowshare,'
while those at the tail cried,
'It's surely a fan.' Others
groping among the legs said
it was more like four pillars
till all were shouting and crying
what the elephant was like . . ."

"But, Donald," I interrupted,
growing impatient now
with this long-winded answer. "Don't
you remember me? I'm
Lizzie. Lizzie Reed, from Springfield."

That seemed to stop the wind
in his throat, for his eyes turned

toward the ground.

"Blind man

to blind man," he muttered,
his voice trailing off in silence,
"it's all plowshares and baskets, once
you've forgotten your face and name."

That ended our conversation.
Curious, unsatisfied,
I tried to recollect
what that blank, cool-shadowed face
reminded me of . . . what . . . who . . .
when all of a sudden it came:
The very look of John Denton
as he sat on a pine bough mat
smoking his pipe. Worn out
from hiking over the mountains
in waist-deep snow, he'd asked
to stay behind the others. When
the next relief party found him
frozen beneath a tree
he looked more calm and content
than any man I'd ever seen.

I finished my shopping early
after that curious encounter
and booked myself a room

in a San Francisco hotel.
But tonight my little pony
wouldn't carry me to where
I wanted to go, for suddenly
I was back in our make-shift cabin
on Donner Lake, the wind
bearing the cries of wolves
through the holes in our tattered shelter.
Mama was boiling ox hides
to a gummy paste by the fire,
and hunger, like a sharp-toothed saw
was gnawing below my heart.
Outside, on the frozen snowcrust
the dead lay scattered—gaunt
and stiff, but more well preserved
than our memories of beef or bread.

Suddenly, a voice cried out, "Relief,
relief!" and we soon found ourselves hiking
over snow fields below bright peaks,
step by weary step, each
dragging through the last man's furrow.
Overhead, the dreaded storm broke
and almost buried us
in swirling drifts. Some wept.
Others stumbled ahead, snow-blind.

Then close in the flurrying distance
I heard the grunting, shuffling
tread of large animals
shambling over the snow—
a file of gray humped elephants
plowed through the steep white drifts.
Pale-gray in the moonlight, each
bore the huddled shape of a body
perched behind the immense head.
Living and dead they came
in grim file, as in a circus:

First, George and Jacob Donner,
and behind them on little calves,
two rows of gaunt-faced children,
and Milt Elliot, that I buried
under the snow with my own hands.
Then Lewis Keseburg, gnawing the bone
of a man he'd killed, smiled down
open-mouthed, baring white teeth,
and behind him, our friend John Denton
smoking his pipe and staring
out of eyes like quartz or ice, while
on his heels, Grandma Keyes
rode high in her four-poster bed.

Up to our desperate camp
they circled and came to a stand—
then one by one their thin voices
called out for me by name.
So weak was I from hunger
I overlooked their strangeness
till my father greeted me,
"Lizzie,
have you read your schoolbooks?"

Then I thought of Hannibal
crossing the Alps, and cried,
"No, Papa, I'm too tired
to take another step. Please
tell me another story."
But by then the mirage had vanished.
I awoke in my dark hotel room
and for nearly half a minute
thought that I, too, had gone blind
till I struck a quick match.

I suppose
that's when it came to me—
how there I lay, an old woman
at the end of a long full life,
whose every day, every minute
since Donner Lake—no, since

first setting out from Springfield—
was a touch of the elephant
no one can see but those
who have walked through snow-covered mountains
hungry, burying their dead
under powder with their own two hands
among neighborly cannibals.
Every hour, every second of
the rest of your life depends
on the next impossible step.
Girlhood, marriage, widowhood
dangle from a spider web!

Then suddenly you're descending
to a California spring. Green
startles your eyes and the sunlight
is almost unbearable.
Wandering off by yourself
to pick wildflowers in Napa Valley,
you hear your father's voice
calling among the hills,
"Come, child, we're ready to start
and you haven't eaten any lunch."

Lunch, after all those days
on the mountain's gray-shadowed flank.

And in the delightful pause
till you answer, the shining
dust of a whole lifetime
trembling like gold in the balance.

Salt

A Grain of Salt

Perhaps on such a day the joke was invented.
It worked to keep us busy for a while.
We'd spent the morning hovering at elbows
or underfoot, until my grandfather,
tired of tipping boards and scattered nails,
told us what then seemed like a miracle—
a magic recipe to catch a bird.
You only had to spread salt on its tail.

To catch a bird with salt!
That was enough
to send us to the woods, clutching sweaty fistfuls
of the elemental grains, and to keep us there
buoyed by hope for one long afternoon
as errant birds flew past to perch in treetops
and the hot sun made our palms grow slick with sweat.

If only they'd come close, we thought. *If only* . . .
But why should knowledge always taste like salt?
We left the woods with one less thieving wish,
wiping our hands off, turning our pockets out.

Revised Standard Version

Sweeping aside the dust of genesis
from molars, femurs, half a fossil skull,
Adam looks back.
                                        There never was a garden.
No snake, no tree. Desire shaped the name
of paradise and gave mankind a mother.

Yet Adam, in his innocence, felt shame
for the creative spirit of this world
who left rough copies riddling the dust
in stony strata throughout Africa.
Jawless, eyeless, they now stare back at him,
bursting thick crania as if to puzzle
their kinship with the dust they're married to—
Australopithecus, Homo erectus,
the whole long lumbering slouch toward sapience
so naked in its brutal mechanisms
Adam must cover it with living green
to fashion its creator in his image.

For even in the dark preserves of Gombe
among his simian cousins, Adam finds
not just a simpler life before agriculture
expelled Eve from a life of gathering,
but circumstantial evidence that crime
is shared, root, branch, and stem, with all creation—
Cannibalism, rape, infanticide,
like thumbs, like hands, the mutual heritage
of apes and men, not shades of mythic Eden
whose fall unstitched the fabric of the world.

Only our human longing for perfection
revised the earth and heavens till they stood
firm above the irremediable
shiftings of chance and chaos. Only man
conceived a perfect earth.

What god or angel,
knowing the stuff of which he'd been compounded
was, form and shape, carved by necessity
and chance and death, would taste such bitter knowl-
edge
and yet, despite its ramifying claims,
still place his minor world among the heavens,
a name among that catalogue of names.

Simon Says

We're playing Simon Says. Remember how?
(Simon says remember how, so it's okay.)
It's not enough to do what Simon says,
It's what he says he says that you obey.
The rules are Simon's. All right, let's begin.
Simon says, Don't read this sentence or you're out.
You did? That's it, game's over, Simon wins,
However much you plead, protest, or pout.
Bound by the iron chain of such curved sense,
Simon himself must discontinue play.
There's no appeal to gray omnipotence.
What Simon says he says he can't unsay.

Eternal Recurrence

What's a blush?
A flicker of hellfire
felt; seen, like sunburn, but,
fortunately, outgrown
like adolescence.
Still, we're not done
with the flesh's mortifications.
Caught with a thumb
up a nostril, or a hand
down our pants,
we're all galled by ourselves.
There you are now, bent double,
bravely feigning indifference
to the lump in your pants —
or flushed, menopausal
in mid sentence, while flirting . . .
To endure that ignominy
again and again.

No wormwood, no brimstone —
hell's a black-tie affair
to which you're invited
accidentally, and come
underdressed, undermannered,
nervous, laughing too loud
between gaffes,

malapropisms,
and badly timed jokes.
There's a black fleck of spinach
wedged between your front teeth,
which you've only just noticed
in the bathroom upstairs,
looking up to glimpse, there,
in the half-drawn-back glass
of the medicine cabinet mirror,
your host's eyes watching you
lightly fingering his things.

Still, it's not over, yet—
it's eternal, remember?
as in that immeasurably
long instant between
the key rattling home in
the lock as you struggle,
handcuffed by shirt sleeves,
pants down past your knees,
and the half second later when
the door opens and
your mouth makes an O. . . .

Then the reel starts again.

The Gift

It is the future generation that presses into
being by means of these exuberant feelings
and supersensible soap bubbles of ours.
—Arthur Schopenhauer

Because we knew that, given half a chance,
Some unknown X or Y might chance to squeeze
Into the world through our exuberance,
With pills and diaphragms and IUD's
We watched the days, marking our calendars
To stem the tide on which the future presses
By riding the crests of kisses and caresses—
Those supersensible soap bubbles of ours.

Because if life's a gift, who's so unkind
As to impose that burden in cold blood?
Philosophers (wrote one) if of sound mind
Should mourn at the existence of this world
Ruled by blind Will, where every chance desire
Torments the soul to act, where to exist
Requires cool logic of the pessimist
Who'd stand unsinged within that blazing fire.

Not to be born: That is the greatest blessing;

The next best, to return from whence you'd come
As soon as possible. . . .
Such second-guessing
Arrives too late: The hero met his doom
Earlier in his life; now old and blind,
He faces death. Despite those who implore us
To cut our losses early in loud chorus,
Instead of doing what they recommend,

Better to recognize that all who walk
On four legs in the morning, two at noon,
And three at evening should ignore loose talk
Of rushing headlong to oblivion
For the sake of mere consistency, to give
The sphinx an answer to her ticklish riddle,
Knowing that while we're stuck here in the middle
Of life, with one imperative—to live—

We're each the center of a tragic play.
We're Oedipus or Hamlet, in Act One,
But by Act Two, hair, beard now going gray,
We've turned to Claudius. Scene follows scene
Until the curtain falls on doddering Lear
Ranting at his own folly. End of drama.
And yet, for all that suffering and trauma,
The smallest gesture's pregnant with grandeur

In the last scene: Fond father and dead child
Move every heart to pity. Purged of terror,
Even blind Oedipus is reconciled
With fate at last, seeing his only error
Was to be tangled in the fatal knot
Of family, like any son of man.
King Laius and Jocasta didn't plan
Such parenthood. Yet though he might regret

The error and the blindness, who could grieve
At being born, when, in his final hour,
Gathering his daughters close and taking leave,
He felt the whole earth shudder with the power
Of God calling him home, felt his heart lift
Over stone fountain, tomb, and sacred grove.
One word alone makes life worth living: Love.
Receive then, child, the gift, yourself a gift.

Additions

No moon, no stars, as if black mirrored black—
The Lords of Darkness sprang to the attack
And folded up in clay the living spark
To populate the kingdom of the dark.

With every birth, the light grows more dispersed
In matter until, totally immersed
And guttering among the planetary spheres,
It dies a heat-death with the universe.

So Mani thought, another misanthrope
Who offered chastity as our one hope
Of stepping off the wheel of death and birth
Till no light's serving time in cells of earth.

Dark, dark, dark, dark. His intellectual betters,
The Greeks, still sometimes saw the light in fetters
Of flesh and bone and with an Orphic guide
Tried to transcend the flesh they'd purified

By abstinence, to head home to the stars
From which, they felt, they'd started their careers.
How consciously to make such grave decisions—
To bring new souls to these dull subdivisions,

To add the extra room, to plan the birth
Of children on this iron-hearted earth—
Iron, the ash of a once-living star.
And yet, like flesh, all light's corpuscular

And propagates itself down living chains.
Even the desert hermit who abstains
From flesh must eat his salad, bite by bite
Consuming, with each morsel, worlds of light.

So cell by cell each infant grows toward day
Till child and sun join in one Milky Way—
Each star, each suburb sweeping back the night.
And every story adds another light.

In a Parking Lot

No use to sit there idling—kill your engine.
I've sat here now myself for fifteen minutes,
Hoping some good Samaritan might slow
And wave me in, but by the time one's noticed,
He's stuck himself across our exit lane.
I give it five more minutes. There you go,
No sense in wasting gas . . . A V-8, right?
I figured. That's the one thing Studebaker
Did right, packing those homely, sawed-off boxes
With the horsepower to take on a Corvette.
You treat it right, that thing will run forever.
So what'd you pay for it? Three hundred bucks?
I guess they saw you coming. Cheer up, though—
Replace the carburetor, give her a tune-up,
And she'll run like a dream, though never look it.
Me, I prefer a Chevy. See this pick-up?
Three hundred thousand miles. My sons and I
Rebuilt it so it's like that famous ax
George Washington used to drop the cherry tree.
See, they replaced the ax-head, then the handle,
And then the head again—each several times—
Insisting that the ax they finished with
Was the same as at the start. Well, that's this truck.
Whatever I didn't fix myself, my sons did
Till all that's left of that first truck's its ghost.
My sons take after me—both born mechanics.

You try your dad—if he's inclined that way,
Together you could fix that clunker up
And have a car to take a girl out in
And not be half ashamed. I know I would.
A father should pass down some kind of knowledge.
My own sons—you could say they worship Pop,
Maybe because I drive a rig. . . . Who knows
Why boys love trucks and truckers like they do?
The last cowboys, some say . . . but trucks aren't horses.
I know—I used to ride mine pretty hard,
And I was a *good* driver. Ask anybody.
I've done things with a truck you wouldn't believe.
Take one time on a joy ride with my boys—
We'd topped this hill and right there down below us
Was a pair of compacts blocking off both lanes.
The only thing I knew to do was jack-knife,
So I hit the brakes and laid that baby down
On the concrete like a kitten curling up
To take a nap—our landing was that easy.
You should have seen my boys climb out the window,
Smiling to see the sky above them now.
The only damage was, I skinned one elbow
On the highway out my window. That and paint.
I've had to lay a rig down more than once
To save an accident and walked away
With nothing more than bruises every time
Except the last.

Now if I'd been some cowboy,
I could have closed my eyes and let that rig

Ride through the fog that night right to our door—
But like I said, a truck's got no horse sense.
I never even saw that station wagon
Till I was right on top of it. You see,
With all that weight behind you, you *can't* stop,
Not when you're pushing eighty, eighty-five.
I think sometimes, though, of that family,
Because, just like I told you, I've got boys.
You must have some yourself . . . But what am I saying?
You're still a kid—you've got a whole lifetime.
Say, look, now that the traffic's letting up,
Here's some advice to send you on your way.
Remember what I said about that car.
The thing to do is, try to keep it up.
Drive careful. It was real nice talking to you.

The Century Killer

The way I had it figured as a kid,
This Mercury would be a relic now
Mounted in some museum, on display
With biplanes, trains, Apollo space capsules
And other tokens of our earthly past.
I never thought that I'd be plowing wind
In one of these old fossil-burning buckets,
Talking to you about such mundane things
As where I went to school or L.A. weather.
I figured that by my age things would change—
Instead of chugging California smog,
We'd live in free fall somewhere deep in space
Beyond the smothering hug of gravity,
Scouting the rings of Saturn, or mining ore
On asteroids, or terraforming Mars
The way experts predicted in my teens.

That's why I hit the road on nights like this
And drive across the desert by myself—
To see the stars so close I might be steering
From world to world across the galaxy
In search of that more habitable world
I first saw pictured then in *Look* and *Life*.
This world is only one of that world's futures.
On other planes, we're living other lives.
Don't ask me how I know.

Tonight, for instance,
I might have dropped you off outside of town
Or passed you by without a second's notice—
And somewhere in their parallel dimensions
Both things are happening simultaneously
With other variations beyond count.

Not here, though. Here you stare up at the sky
As I drive toward that distant nebula
Of lights, as if there were no other selves
Converging and diverging at each crossroad.
We've gained solidity, like stone or bone.
I've fleshed us out like the textbook illustrations
I meditated on in junior college,
Projecting myself backward into time
Like the hero in a science fiction novel
Until I reached my goal, the late Stone Age,
And moved among those fur-clad men and women
Clutching their polished bone and stone-chipped tools
Until a cough or shuffle fetched me back
To night school and my dull instructor's voice.

I envied them their savage innocence,
Their fearless hearts.
Imagine setting out
Without sails, maps, or compasses to claim
Every continent and two-bit desert island
From here to Bimini and the North Pole,
Trusting the wind to toss your starving party

Onto a sandy void a world away.
And then to settle down and make a life
Complete with language, gods, and table manners
Out of an empty waste. . . .

We couldn't do it.
We've lost ourselves beneath a tottering pile
Of histories and myths and languages—
Greek, Latin, French—the things an English schoolboy
Was forced to learn—then math, computers, science. . . .
It got too much for anyone to stand!
That's what I saw. It only needed courage
To give the thing a push and let it topple.
So much for dreams, so much for science fiction.
Here's where we are forever—shrunken, small,
And lost beneath a scattering of stars
We'll never visit, growing thick and heavy.

That's why I never tried to finish school.
I saw we'd lost the simple elegance
Of hand axes and deftly whittled bone
And that the best that we could hope for now
Would be a kind of throwback to that time—
A tire iron simple as a thigh bone,
A chromed and thundering chariot of a car,
And in the place of virgin continents
And chartless seas, a four lane interstate
To guide the modern hunter to his prey.
There, if a man could find it in himself

To free his mind and conscience from their shackles,
He could renew himself, again and again,
Washing the soot of time away with blood
And reemerging pure, anonymous,
And stripped of all civilizing inhibitions
That shrink and weigh him down.

I had a teacher
Back at that school who always used to say
That good and evil were only categories
And that if we could step outside their bounds
Just once, we'd see things in another light.
He was an atheist, with two small daughters
Framed on his desk, for all his heady talk,
And stuttered when I told him of my plan—
Though why, if there's no God and good and evil
Are merely mind-projected categories
Any of it should shock.

What is surprising
Is how the open highway swallows hours
And turns them into miles, not keeping count,
Whatever happens, so even I lose track
Of what I tried to drive into his head
A half a life ago, or why it matters
To tell it to you now as we approach
The outer edge of Phoenix, except to say
A certain peace comes in the telling of it—
I'm not sure why—and afterwards I feel

Weightless, serene . . . as if this Mercury
Were like its namesake, god of roads and thieves,
And I had all the time that ever was
Or ever will be pressed between my palms:

I roll it in a ball and then I squeeze.

Two Hitchhikers

Once driving down a dark stretch of state highway
Through moonless countryside, not far from home,
Our headlights caught, as in a flashbulb's flare,
A pair of hitchhikers:

One held a crutch
More than he leaned against it, and the other . . .
But the negative dissolved as we swept past.
I felt the car lurch right (my friend was driving)
As the brakes took hold, then they were getting in
To the back seat. Both reeked of beer and whiskey.

"Say, why don't you boys drive us down to Midway
To get some beer. . . . They kicked us out the bar."

"We're going the other way," my friend protested.
"We'll drop you on our way, just tell us where."

That silenced them—that is, until we slowed
At a stop sign at the next dark intersection,
And when they spoke, it was with more than words.
I heard a sudden snickering of steel,
Then saw the knife blade nipping my friend's ribs
As he clutched the wheel, and sensed near my own chin
The warm unsteady hand poised at my throat
And just the slightest kiss of silvery blade.
"Turn here," the one without the crutch commanded,
So we made a U-turn there and headed south.

That made them cordial. Putting away their knives,
One lounged across the back seat, one leaned forward
To share a joke, all beery fellowship,
And to pass the time, kept up a steady patter
For several miles.

"Say, you boys must be hippies—
I seen them beards. Well, hell, we're just like you—
We want some beer so we can go and get dizzy. . . ."
And so on, always ending in the refrain,
"We're like you boys, we only want to get dizzy.
Yeah, we smoke pot . . . and marijuana, too!"

After twenty miles, they both seemed harmless
enough—
Relatively, I mean, with their knives tucked in their
coats—
And since we had to, in a funny way,
We warmed up to them till we had to stop.

Then things got complicated. They got confused—
Should they leave us there while they went in to shop?
Of course not—we'd drive off and leave them stranded.
One stay with us, one knife against us two,
While one went in?
They didn't like that either.

At last, they hit upon the expedient:
They'd walk in single file, one behind each,
Hands in their pockets, fingering their knives,

And, after dire threats, so we paraded
Around the store, then through the check-out line.

I've told this story a hundred times, I know,
And always left out how we bought that six-pack,
Ashamed of how I'd sheepishly been steered
Out to the car, to get back in again
With our abductors. Because it seemed cowardly
Not to have clutched a magnum of champagne
And clubbed one over the head, crying bloody mur-
 der—
Or at least to have leapt a shelf of cut-rate gin
And waited for fireworks. Liquor stores have guns.

Instead, I skip right to the funny ending:
How after we'd retraced the same dark road
To where we'd picked them up, they made us turn
Suddenly off onto a dead-end lane
Along which three lights shone from three dark shacks.
We passed the first, the second, approached the third,
And just as we faced the woods where I envisioned
Our last life-and-death struggle or breakneck flight,
A voice said, "Turn in here," and they got out—
It must have been their house—and turning toward us,
Reached in a pocket, pulled out two dollar bills
And muttering, "Here, this is for your gas,"
Turned back around and lurched into the house.

We locked the doors and burned that dirt road up
Getting out of there. . . .

That's how the tale might end.

But seeing them in the store's bright parking lot
Confused and half afraid of us, scraggly and scrawny,
One gimp-legged, both "just wanting to get dizzy,"
But without a car to fetch their beer back home,
I guess we thought that it would be less trouble
To trust our lives to their humanity,
Or luck—and, anyway, all made it home.

As we spun out to the hard-topped county road,
My friend reached out and handed me one dollar.
"Here, you've earned half of this."

We couldn't stop laughing.

That's how a tale should end—in dizzying laughter,
Though some won't be arranged to end that way.

Notes on the Poems

The factual parts of the poem, "Seeing the Elephant", are based on a narrative by Elizabeth Reed Murphy entitled "Across the Plains in the Donner Party," published in *Century*, XLII (1891). In a few brief passages I have borrowed her wording, slightly altering it where necessary.

"One of the recurrent phrases on almost every lip during America's period of western expansion was 'seeing the elephant.' The phrase had various shades of meaning—to see the sights, to gain experience of life—but in the main, seeing the elephant meant going west with one's eyes wide open, expecting to find marvels and wondrous fortunes only to be monstrously defrauded in the end."

—Dee Brown, *The Gentle Tamers*

About the Author

Paul Lake's first poetry collection, *Another Kind of Travel*, received the Porter Fund Award for Literary Excellence. His essays on poetry have appeared widely in journals and anthologies. His novel *Among the Immortals* (Story Line), a satirical thriller about poets and vampires, was picked as one of the best first novels by The Year's Best Fantasy and Horror. Lake is currently a professor of English and Creative Writing at Arkansas Tech University and lives in Russellville with his wife, artist Tina Lake, and their two children.